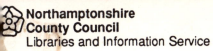

Skeletons and Movement

written by Maria Gordon
and
illustrated by Mike Gordon

Wayland

Simple Science

Air

Colour

Day and Night

Electricity and Magnetism

Float and Sink

Heat

Light

Materials

Push and Pull

Rocks and Soil

Skeletons and Movement

Sound

Series Editor: Catherine Baxter

Advice given by Audrey Randall – member of the Science Working Group
for the National Curriculum.

First published in 1995 by
Wayland (Publishers) Ltd
61 Western Road, Hove
East Sussex, BN3 1JD, England

British Library Cataloguing in Publication Data
Gordon, Maria
    Skeletons and Movement. – (Simple Science Series)
    I. Title II. Gordon, Mike III. Series
    535.6

ISBN 0-7502-1598-4

Typeset by MacGuru
Printed and bound in Italy by G Canale and C.S.p.A., Turin, Italy

Contents

A skeleton is the hard part of a body which keeps it stiff. A skeleton gives a body its shape. It keeps the soft, inside parts safe.

Touch your knees and elbows. You are feeling parts of your skeleton. They feel hard and strong under your skin.

Without a skeleton, your body would be like a big sack of jelly!

Your skeleton is inside your body. It is called an endo-skeleton. Look at the hard bits that are left when a fish or roast chicken is eaten. These bits are parts of an endo-skeleton.

Endo-skeletons have lots of parts joined together. Most are made of bone.

Bone is hard on the outside, light, and strong. Feel a chicken bone. Ask a grown-up to cut it in half. Look and poke inside.

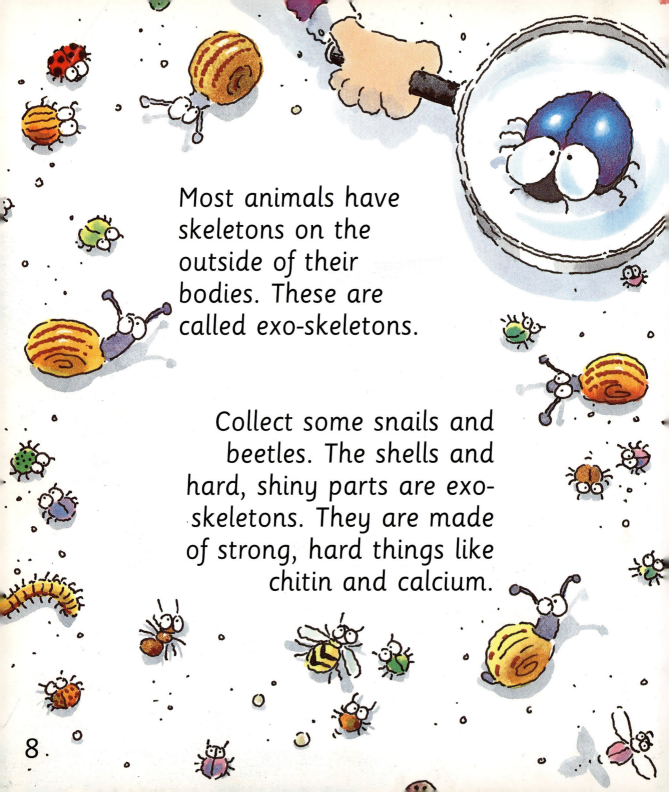

Most animals have skeletons on the outside of their bodies. These are called exo-skeletons.

Collect some snails and beetles. The shells and hard, shiny parts are exo-skeletons. They are made of strong, hard things like chitin and calcium.

8

Animals like tortoises have exo-skeletons and endo-skeletons.

Animals like worms, slugs and squids don't have skeletons at all!

YIKES!

When animals and people die, their skeletons last longer than the soft parts of their bodies.

9

Cave people learnt to use parts of skeletons as knives, arrowheads, scrapers, jewellery and even musical instruments.

Many people still believe bones hold magic too.

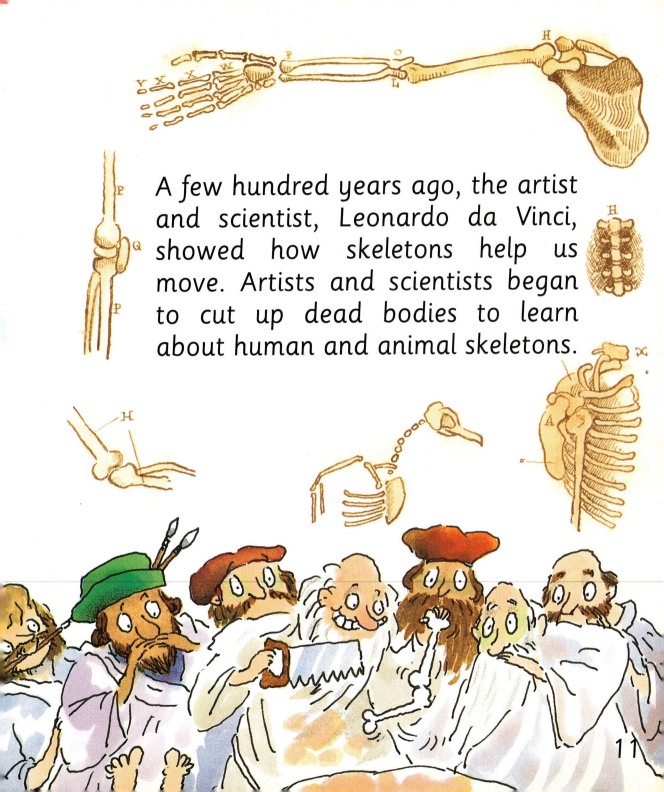

A few hundred years ago, the artist and scientist, Leonardo da Vinci, showed how skeletons help us move. Artists and scientists began to cut up dead bodies to learn about human and animal skeletons.

11

Animals without skeletons, and animals with exo-skeletons cannot grow very big. If they did, they would get too heavy to move.

Look at some shells. These are the exo-skeletons of molluscs. They get bigger as the molluscs grow inside.

Many exo-skeletons cannot grow. The animals inside them have to leave them behind! This is called shedding. The animal makes a new skeleton underneath. This goes hard when the old one is shed. Look for shed spider skeletons. They look like dead spiders.

All skeletons are made so animals can move. Different skeletons help animals move in different ways.

Ask an adult to help. Trace this shape on to card, cut it out and fold it. Cut out the circles. Put your fingers through the holes and make them walk.

14

Your fingers make the shape move. They are like a tortoise's legs or a boxfish's fins.

The softer, moving parts poke out through the exo-skeleton.

15

Skeletons have joints. Joints are the places where bones or other hard parts meet. Different ways of moving need different joints.

Some animals have exo-skeletons made of hard plates. The parts where the plates meet are thin and bendy.

Cut a long strip of stiff card about 5 cm wide. It does not bend easily.

Now cut it into parts as shown.

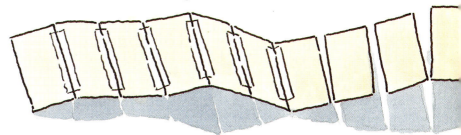

These are like plates. Tape all the parts back together. Now the strip is very bendy.

This is like a scorpion's tail or a lobster's tummy.

Feel how your back can bend and twist. Feel the bumps down the middle of your back. This is your backbone.

The bumps are bones joined together. They are called vertebrae.

Animals with backbones are called vertebrates.

Animals without backbones are called invertebrates.

Bend and twist a closed zip.
Your vertebrae lock together
a bit like the teeth of the zip.
They have sliding joints. This
makes your backbone bendy.

20

Bend your knee. It has two bones joined together.

The joint between your foot and your ankle moves like a door on a hinge. This is also how a cockle shell opens and closes. It has a hinge joint.

Swing your arm around. It is joined to your shoulder. The joint is a ball and socket joint.

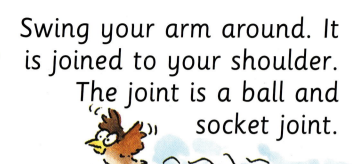

Make a ball of silver foil to fit an eggcup. The eggcup is a kind of socket. Poke in a lolly stick as shown. Now stir the ball in the eggcup.

This is how the bone at the top of your arm moves.

Some bones are joined so they cannot move. Many brains have a bony cover called a skull. Tap your head. You are feeling bones that have grown together. They keep your brain safe and make sure it doesn't move too much.

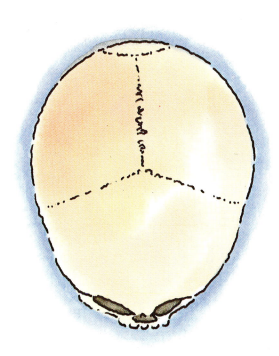

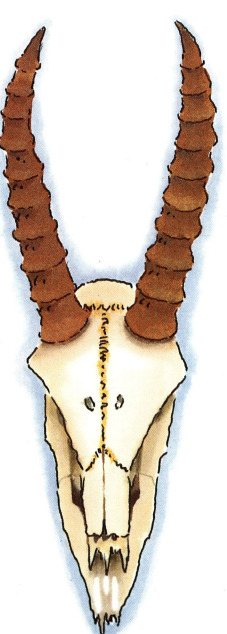

Many bones are joined to muscles. Feel the soft parts around your arms and legs. These are muscles. Muscles pull on bones at joints and make them move.

Ask an adult to help. Cut out two bone shapes like these from stiff card.

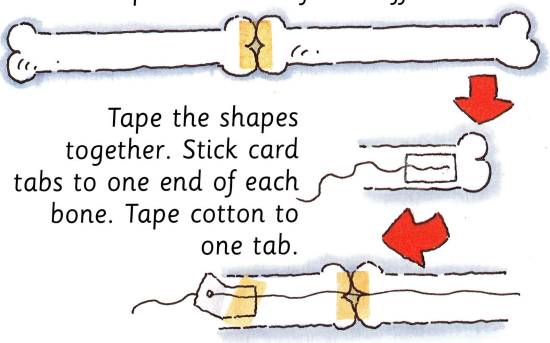

Tape the shapes together. Stick card tabs to one end of each bone. Tape cotton to one tab.

Thread the end through the other tab. Pull the cotton.

The cotton is like a muscle pulling up a bone. Your model is like a hinge joint.

Even beetles have muscles in their legs.
Muscles help mouths, beaks and shells to
open. They make wings flap and
claws pinch and dig.

Look at these skeletons.

Fish skeletons show they
do not walk.

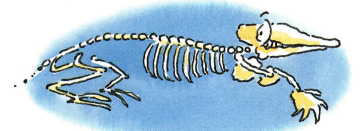

Mole bones show that moles dig.

Frog skeletons show
frogs can jump.

Pteranodon bones
even show that
pteranodons flew!

Your skeleton helps you run and walk...sit and stand... jump and dance.

Even if it breaks, a healthy skeleton can mend very well.

Good food and lots of exercise help skeletons
stay strong and healthy. How do you like to
keep your skeleton moving?

Notes for adults

The 'Simple Science' series helps children to reach Key Stage 1: Attainment Targets 1-4 of the Science National Curriculum.

Below are some suggestions to help complement and extend the learning in this book.

4/5   Relate bones to a real or model human skeleton. Explore man-made structures and their framework, from steel inside concrete to coat hangers. Look at protective packaging such as egg boxes.

6/7   Compare shark skeletons – made of cartilage, as found in human ears and noses. Scoop out bone marrow. Discuss the link between bones and blood. Make fish bone prints. Do the Okie Cokie!

8/9   Look at coats of mail. Compare menus and diets from different cultures – which 'meat' items, from beef to snails, have exo- versus endo-skeletons?

10/11   Look at religious relics and museum exhibits of bone and shell implements. Read the Greek myth of Jason fighting the skeleton warriors. Research symbols from skull and crossbones to poison warnings and tattoos. Make an art display including da Vinci, and Stubbs' work on horses. Visit a graveyard.

12/13   Compare snakes to worms. Discuss human growth, comparing baby clothes with current ones. Show dust as shed skin sample. Make size charts contrasting animals with endo/exo skeletons. Show how water allows for bigger skeletons.

14/15   Look at skeletal differences such as hollow bones of flying birds and jaws of carnivores versus plant eaters. Do P.E. Measure speed of movement. Read 'The Tortoise and the Hare'.

16/17   Put stickers on every joint spotted – in people, woodwork, toys, etc. Visit an orthopaedic hospital department. Borrow a used cast. Survey handicap provisions.

18/19	Investigate standard patterns of skeletons – backbones, ribs, limbs, etc. Compare movement of vertebrates and invertebrates.
20/21	Watch acrobats and gymnasts. Hold a three-legged race.
22/23	Borrow a hip replacement joint. Look at the unfused bones on a baby's head.
24/25	Display anatomical diagrams. Show how muscles work in pairs. Ask a butcher for a chicken's foot – show effect of pulling a tendon. Talk about voluntary versus involuntary movements, from hearts beating to eyes blinking.
26/27	Look at skeletal remains in owl pellets. Invent an animal and write a story about it. Design a skeleton to suit its movements. Investigate sculpture and crime-lab skull reconstructions.
28/29	Look at X-rays. Investigate link between diet and height, rickets, etc. Make a photographic display showing everyone busy at their favourite sport/dance activity.

Other books to read

Healthy Food by A. Qualter & J Quinn (Wayland, 1993)

Moving by Joy Richardson (Hodder & Stoughton, 1991)

Skeletons & Movement by K. Davies & W. Oldfield, (Wayland, 1991)

Index